D1094566

TAKASAKI MASAHARU

TAKASAKI MASAHARU

An Architecture of Cosmology

Princeton Architectural Press, New York

Published by
Princeton Architectural Press
37 East 7th Street
New York, New York 10003
212.995.9620

For a free catalog of books, call 1.800.722.6657
Visit our web site at www.papress.com

Editing and design: Clare Jacobson
Special thanks to: Eugenia Bell, Jane Garvie,
Caroline Green, Therese Kelly, Mark Lamster,
Anne Nitschke, and Sara E. Stemen
—Kevin C. Lippert, publisher

Library of Congress Cataloging-in-Publication Data
Takasaki, Masaharu, 1953–
    Takasaki Masaharu : an architecture of cosmology.
       p.   cm.
    Includes bibliographical references.
    ISBN 1-56898-121-X (alk. paper)
    1. Takasaki, Masaharu, 1953– . 2. Architecture,
Modern—20th century—Japan. I. Title.
    NA 1559.T235A4 1998
    720'.92—dc21   97-22469
                                                   CIP

Frontispiece
Tamana City Observatory Museum, 1992
photo ©Yoshio Takase, GA Photographers

Photo credits
©Satoshi Asakawa: 50, 51b, 53c, 58
©Isao Imbe: 60, 64b, 65, 68tr, 74, 76, 77t, 78, 79
©Hajime Inoue, Fukuoka Style: 127
©Toshihisa Ishii, Shotenkenchiku-sha: 82–84, 86,
87, 92, 95
©Yoshihiko Kabayama: 13r, 34, 35t, 36, 37, 38t, 40,
43b, 137b, 140b, 141
©Katsuhisa Kida: 13l, 98, 99tl, 109, 126b
©Satoru Mishima: 64t
©Tomio Ohashi: 146, 147
©Hans Sautter, Pacific Press Service: 10r, 11r, 16,
18b, 28, 30–33, 35b, 38b, 39, 42, 43t, 67, 68tl
©Shinkenchiku-sha: 10l, 11l, 12l, 18t, 19–23, 26, 27,
49, 51tl, 51tr, 52, 53l, 53r, 54, 55, 62, 63l, 66, 68b, 69,
77b, 80, 85, 90, 91, 93, 94, 96, 99tr, 99b, 100–03, 106,
110t, 111t, 112–15, 116t, 117, 119, 123, 124, 125b, 126tl,
126tr, 128–31, 134–36, 137tl, 137tc, 138, 139, 142, 143,
148, 149, 154
©Shokokusha Photographers: 150, 151
©Takasaki Masaharu Architects: 44, 152, 153, 155–57
©Yoshio Takase, GA Photographers: 46–48, 59, 63r,
70, 71, 75
©Hiroshi Ueda, GA Photographers: 12r, 107t, 108b,
110b, 111b
©Tohru Waki, Shokokusha: 107b, 108t, 116b, 118,
122, 125t, 137tr, 140t

CONTENTS

9 Introduction, Botond Bognar

16 Crystal Light

28 Zero Cosmology

44 Tamana City Observatory Museum

60 Earth Architecture

80 Aso-Kuju National Park Restaurant

96 Kihoku Astronomical Museum

112 Shomyo Kindergarten

128 Takasaki Masaharu Museum of Architecture

145 Projects

INTRODUCTION

An Architecture of the Unknown and the Unknowable

Botond Bognar

I have been [investigating] architecture as a social art since 1982. By creating a happy blending of people and things, I see my challenge as that of trying to marry materials and spirit via an internal dynamic force....I would like to address the voices of primitiveness, nature, humanity, and divinity [in] molding [architecture] and [designing] space....I also believe that architecture should recreate our relationship with spiritual things, defining its new direction.

Takasaki Masaharu[1]

Born in 1953, Takasaki Masaharu belongs to a generation of Japanese architects whose activities were launched during the so-called "bubble economy" in the 1980s, a time that was conducive to extensive experimentation in architecture and urbanism. It is not surprising that the works of this new generation display an unusually broad spectrum of design directions; in this regard they seem to match and perhaps even surpass those of their immediate predecessors, including Tadao Ando, Toyo Ito, Itsuko Hasegawa, Kiko Mozuna, Team Zoo, Riken Yamamoto, and Shin Takamatsu. These architects, representing the first post-Metabolist (post-Modern) generation, introduced a fundamentally new, pluralistic architecture and set the tone of design for future generations of Japanese architects.

Takasaki's work, however, is largely unparalleled not only within the extremely varied field of Japanese architecture, but also within today's world of architecture at large. His work stands out from that of his contemporaries because his powerfully imaginative, truly fantastic, and highly idiosyncratic designs are less concerned with the acceleration of urban culture and the vagaries of Japanese urbanism; instead they draw inspiration and energy from other, often mythical sources and mysterious powers and are preoccupied with far larger, usually cosmic dimensions. Indeed, for Takasaki nothing is really simple and no issue is a small matter.

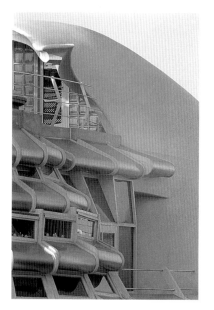

Crystal Light, 1987
Zero Cosmology, 1991

As the name of his office—Mono-Bito Institute—and his credo indicate, Takasaki, while regarding architecture as a social art, seeks to mediate between things or objects (*mono*) and humans or subjects (*bito*), as much as between spirituality and materiality. Yet Takasaki's rather optimistic posture and social agenda, strategies that Modern architects likewise advocated, are coupled in his work with an anti-Modern attitude, namely an intuitive, nonrational, and highly spiritual approach to design that occasionally recollects the primitive in architecture. This means that his designs tend to be more organically than technologically oriented. Nevertheless they rely on meticulous craftsmanship and frequently, as well as paradoxically, necessitate the application of sophisticated technologies.[2] What seems to emerge from his designs then is a new, holistic order guiding the relationship between people and their world. This order, while maintaining the belief that architecture can still shape society, is unfettered by the dichotomies of old and new, earthly and cosmic, natural and man-made, and so on, and has equally nothing to do with the rationale in which Modern "social engineering" was pursued.

My initial encounter with Takasaki's work came in visiting his first built project, Crystal Light (1987), a small guest house in Tokyo, which elicited much attention and praise from many Japanese architects, including Toyo Ito. The strange building featuring curving lines, molded surfaces, stainless-steel membranes, metallic and glass screens, and a huge egg-shaped corner element alluded as much to some futuristic device as to a prehistoric creature whose world can only exist in the imagination.

Yet, Crystal Light can remind the observer of Gunther Domenig's Favoriten branch of the Central Municipal Bank (1979) in Vienna (Takasaki worked with Domenig for a few years in the early 1980s) or Antonio Gaudi's Casa Mila (1910) in Barcelona (where somewhat similarly undulating or "melted" organic forms shape the building). Crystal Light, although the first

Tamana City Observatory Museum, 1992
Earth Architecture, 1994

step on the road to Takasaki's more recent and more profoundly personal architecture, carries many elements of his unfolding vision of the world and, as such, remains a very important project in his overall work.

In the 1990s Takasaki's architecture expanded in both scope and volume with projects built mainly in Kyushu, in particular around Kagoshima-shi, where he now lives and also works; he maintains a branch office there in addition to his main office in Tokyo. In 1996 on a trip to Kyushu I had the chance to meet Takasaki and visit several of his recent buildings. The visit revealed that his thinking and architecture are rooted in the lush, almost tropical, and extremely rich natural landscape of southern Japan and are influenced by the culture and friendly nature of its people. The trip also provided me with a rare experience; in our age of pressing efficiency, instrumental rationalism, and spiritual deprivation, one seldom comes across an architect with the creative imagination, the unique ability, and the strong commitment to create works that can conjure up archaic yet uniquely new, alien yet strangely familiar, unexpected yet inviting worlds.

As if shaped by natural and atavistic forces through the hands of a magician or shaman who could tame them, Takasaki's buildings radiate a magnetic energy that captivates even the skeptic. Sometimes tortured, fragmented, and scattered, the apparently chaotic forms of his creations—buildings, structures, and unbuilt projects alike—bring to life biomorphic organisms, which are held together in a mysterious way. Takasaki's designs seem to answer to an altogether different kind of logic, proving that the rational is merely one among the orders guiding our world.

The unusually animated forms of Takasaki's architecture stem from a profoundly holistic mode of thinking in which logic is "fuzzy" rather than linear or instrumental. Many of his designs include not only some uniquely shaped "antennae"—which I would call "space sensors"[3]—but also the form

Aso-Kuju National Park Restaurant, 1994
Kihoku Astronomical Museum, 1995

and structural shell of a large nested egg, whose space Takasaki refers to as "zero cosmology."[4] Such an interior is indeed like a cosmic womb pregnant with the seed of another world that is not yet fully evolved but that is to be born or, perhaps, reborn. It breeds an unnamed originator—a genesis of a world with or within an amorphous space, which cannot be ordered by the rules of everyday perception and the one-point perspective. Indeed, Takasaki's work recollects and presents in a *new* light the *unperspective* paradigm of traditional Japanese art and architecture.[5]

Takasaki has written, "[Works of] architecture should land on Earth as if they came from a far universe."[6] In other words, his works, "cosmic" in origin, are intended to be messengers between earth and sky, microcosms and macrocosms, as well as past and future, science and mythology; they also are intended to act as curious mirrors in which we humans can catch a rare glimpse of not only the mysteries of the universe, but also of ourselves. The model for this architecture is not the mechanistic world of the machine, but that of Takasaki's understanding of the order and organism of nature, life, and the universe.

While unique, Takasaki's magical and often ritualistic world invites comparison to others with similar intentions and destination. It is akin to Rudolf Steiner's philosophy of anthroposophy and his architecture of Goetheanum at Dornach (1928). It also shows affinity with the playful designs of the Japanese group Team Zoo, and even more so with the Hungarian Imre Makovecz's organic, vernacular-inspired, and highly mythical works that Makovecz, like Takasaki, calls "building beings." Ultimately, their philosophies can be traced back to Eastern animism, which, in Takasaki's case, is represented by Shinto, a traditional pantheistic Japanese religion.

The close connection between Takasaki's work and these ancient, and occasionally prevailing, sources is poignantly demonstrated by such designs

Shomyo Kindergarten, 1995
Takasaki Masaharu Museum of Architecture, 1996

as his Energy Earth in Nagoya (1988), Cosmos of Chizu in Tottori (1991), and Shomyo Kindergarten in Kagoshima (1995). In these examples the use and articulation of wooden structures leave no doubt that Takasaki's work links nature and artifice. It is important to note that while the works of many contemporary architects, both in Japan and abroad, seek the inspiration of nature and engage it in various ways, they can rarely be described as "organic." On the other hand, Takasaki's work—even when molded in reinforced concrete, as most of his outstanding projects are—are unmistakably organic, beyond their "cosmic origin"; the organic and the cosmic form an inseparable whole while giving a new existential meaning to his architecture.

Experiencing the magical world of Takasaki's architecture, as represented for example by his Tamana City Observatory Museum (1992), Kihoku Astronomical Museum (1995), and large Community Center for the Aged in Ibusuki (1998, now under construction), evokes the awe that one feels when looking at images taken by the Hubbell Telescope about the unimaginable nexus and depths of the universe; it is the experience of coming face to face with the infinity and timelessness of the cosmos, the inexplicable and the unexplainable, that is, the dimensions of the unknown and unknowable. Indeed, Takasaki's works are hard to define or categorize; they demand a kind of knowing whose goal is not to define the world in absolute certainties or as an unimpeachable reality, but as a continuously unfolding, fluid, living phenomenon. As Chris Fawcett noted, such designs "serve to remind us that categorization is only a very small step towards an understanding of architecture, which at its greatest depth must remain unnameable, and unknown."[7]

NOTES

1 Takasaki Masaharu, in his credo as it appears on his letterhead and business cards.

2 Such designs as the Tamana City Observatory Museum (1992), the Kihoku Astronomical Museum (1995), and other uniquely shaped, reinforced concrete structures require complex construction technologies and use no prefabricated elements; they are molded entirely on the site.

3 "Space" is used here in its cosmic rather than architectural sense.

4 Takasaki Masaharu, *Zero Cosmology*, unpublished manuscript provided by the author.

5 The conception of traditional Japanese architecture, urbanism, and art is devoid of the rules of perspective that, discovered or "invented" in Renaissance Europe, became the foundation of individualism and the Western "objective" world view of a well-defined center occupied by the human subject. This mode of representation was largely missing in Japan until the middle of the nineteenth century. Takasaki's mysteriously and wonderfully complex, fragmentary, and even "chaotic" designs and spatial matrices, often eschewing the rules of orthogonal geometry, are ordered with a different sensibility and, as such, are close to a non-perspective paradigm of architecture (and understanding of the world).

6 Takasaki, *Zero Cosmology*.

7 Chris Fawcett, *The New Japanese House* (New York: Harper and Row Publishers, 1980), 165.

WORKS

CRYSTAL LIGHT

Shibuya-ku
Tokyo-to
1987

Crystal Light is an architectural work that provokes its viewers' artistic impulses. I intend the building to inspire a person's body, mind, and spirit to freely take flight, consciously or unconsciously. The building serves as a catalyst to help people link their will to make forms to the "will" of the materials to be made into forms.

I consider architecture to be a social art. It is an act of form making that realizes people's views on the cosmos, nature, and themselves, that recognizes a past history while producing new forms, that is created and re-created as if it were a living creature, that balances its physical structure and its functional mechanisms, and that allows the infinite world contained in the universe to resound.

Actually, in designing architecture, I take into consideration not only social elements, such as the sensitivity and emotional development of the users, the value of handmade products, and the incorporation of community characteristics, but also individual elements, such as the innate forms of nature and the subconscious conceptions of human beings. I attempt to design an architectural work as a "social being" containing these social elements, and as a "living entity" implicitly expressing these individual elements. Architecture should relate with nature as a whole, as well as to mental and spiritual aspects of people in the community. Through such formative art, I intend to exert some impact on a new culture or new consciousness.

Architectural forms are closely related to their community and their environment—they are "second nature," so to speak. Architecture also enhances the cultural, educational, and working environments of the community as a part of its social assets. All kinds of art should aim at giving people a chance to communicate, share feelings, and rejoice in their daily lives. They should make new types of social interactions, generate spiritual consonance, and present an energy of sensitivity.

View from the east

RIGHT *Ring of louvers covering the patio*
BELOW *View from south*
FACING PAGE *Detail view from southwest*

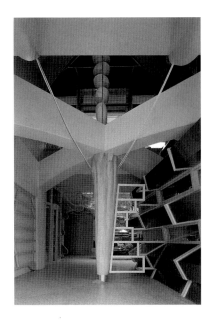

FACING PAGE *Detail of west corner*
ABOVE *Detail of main entrance*
LEFT *Stainless steel eaves in front of main entrance*

FOLLOWING PAGES
LEFT *View up from patio*
RIGHT *View down toward patio*

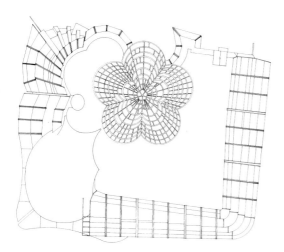

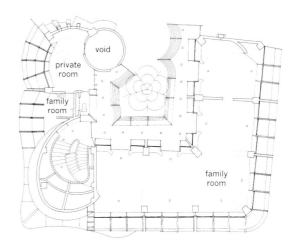

TOP LEFT *Roof plan*
TOP RIGHT *Third floor plan*
CENTER *Second floor plan*
BOTTOM *First floor plan*

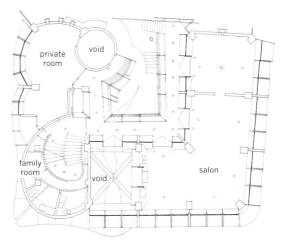

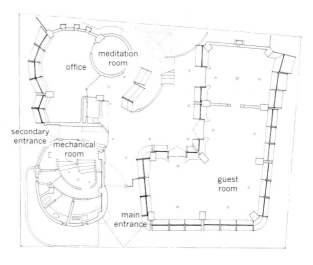

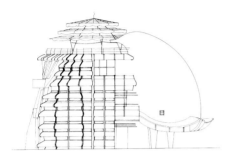

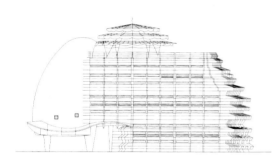

TOP *Southeast elevation*
CENTER LEFT *Northeast elevation*
CENTER RIGHT *Southwest elevation*
BOTTOM LEFT *Northeast section*
BOTTOM RIGHT *Southwest section*

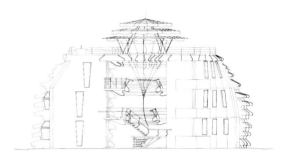

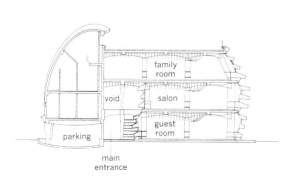

family
room

void   salon

parking   guest
room

main
entrance

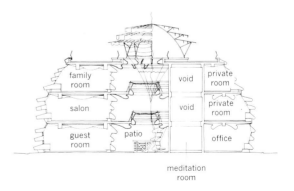

family   void   private
room   room

salon   void   private
                          room

guest   patio   office
room

meditation
room

ABOVE *View toward interior of guest room*
RIGHT *Japanese cypress column at entrance to guest room*

FAR LEFT *Inviting door*
LEFT *View up into stairwell*
BELOW *Office*

ZERO COSMOLOGY

In Kagoshima-ken, which lies at the southwest tip of Japan, there is a volcanic mountain range consisting of the Sakurajima, Kirishima, and Kaimondake mountains, which symbolize the dynamism of the place. The East China Sea is to the west, the Pacific Ocean to the southeast, and a large number of big and small islands to the south, all of which demand attention. The calm ocean, like a mirror of still water, keeps the volcanic energy deep underground, while the peculiar land form, which relates the various energies of fire, earth, and water, emits a spiritual essence.

Kagoshima is a sacred place. One could imagine from its topography that it is linked to the myths of ancient times; it is a place where ancient shamanism still lives. People have an intuitive feeling about such a place—a feeling similar to that when one's conscious is beaten or soul is shaken by the appearance of a sacred phantom. Land that is reminiscent of ancient times can penetrate a hardened current civilization.

I searched for an architecture suitable for such a sacred place. The center of Zero Cosmology, based on the shape of a rotated zero, is a universal symbol of eternal life. The floating feeling of the interior makes the architecture seem as if it has flown in from the future. The architecture exists in the present, but it is absent from this era and goes to other places or times. The appearance of architecture must not only address its existence in the present but also its existence in history.

There are many places in Kagoshima that show its strong mind, but I located Zero Cosmology at a site that yearns for the original topography. In Kagoshima ancient times exist alongside the present, denying the existence of a super modernism. The ancient energy also connects to the future, just as the energy in the volcano range has an inner rhythm of returning to the past and moving to the future concurrently. The history of Kagoshima has not been completed.

Interior view of space of zero; natural light falls down from fifty-four windows

ABOVE *View of Zero Cosmology within its neighborhood*
RIGHT *View from south*
FACING PAGE *View from south toward Sakurajima volcano*

FACING PAGE *Detail of top of zero form*
RIGHT *Detail of top of zero form*
FAR RIGHT *View of zero form from southwest*
BELOW *View from west over a typical Japanese* kawara *roof*

FACING PAGE *View of deity place at balcony*
LEFT *View of zero form from third floor*
BELOW *View up into zero form*

FACING PAGE *Floating base of zero form;
the feet of abstract rabbits stretch to the
center of place of water*
BELOW *View of place of water from an air
hole in the floor of space of zero*

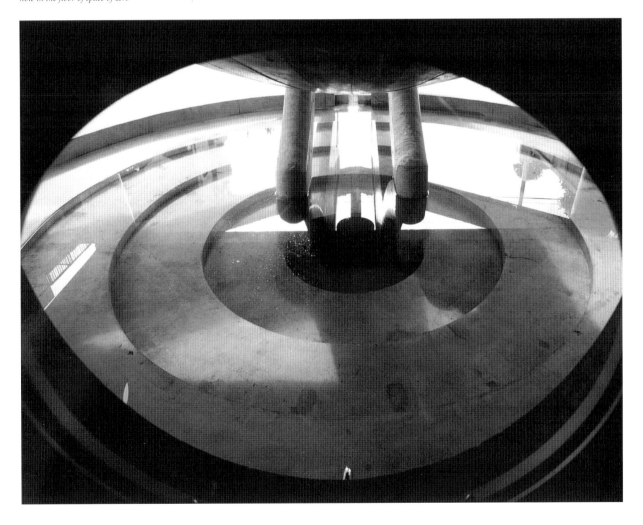

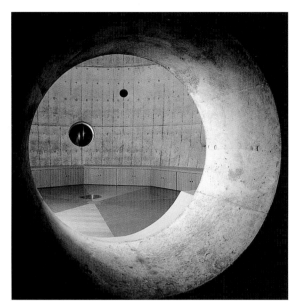

LEFT *Entrance of space of zero*
BELOW *Interior of space of zero*
FACING PAGE *View from interior of space of zero toward entrance*

void

balcony

bedroom

bathroom

space of zero

hall

kitchen

room of
essence

place
of sun

place of water

entrance

storage

music
room

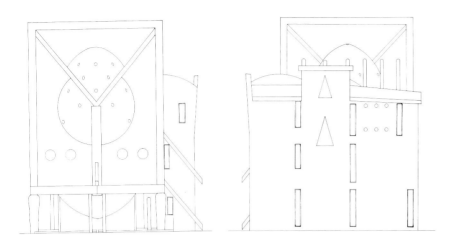

FACING PAGE *third, second, and first floor plans; view to base of space of zero*
THIS PAGE, CLOCKWISE *south, north, and east elevations; section*

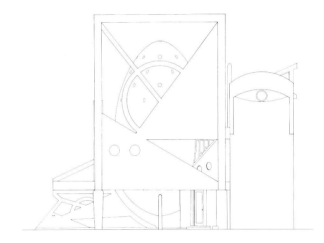

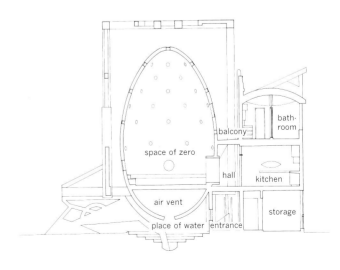

FACING PAGE *Spaceman Plaza at top of stairway*
LEFT *Entrance to third floor bedroom*
BELOW *Staircase on second floor*

TAMANA CITY
OBSERVATORY MUSEUM

Tamana
Kumamoto·ken
1992

The Tamana City Observatory Museum is an exposed concrete observation deck standing on the top of a hill in the center of a sports park. In both its exterior and interior designs, ninety-degree angles have been avoided, and an organic form has been created to respond to minute variations of light, wind, and other elements of nature.

The structure is divided into three phases. The *chinoza* (earth room) on the first floor is a boat-shaped plaza-type space that responds to both the energy bubbling up from the ground and that falling from the sky. It was designed to be a location where city residents could socialize. On the second floor, the *kumonoza* (cloud room) is a space designed to give visitors an experience of the attitudes and outlook of city residents and the pride expressed in their slogan, "Our Tamana." From here there are wonderful views looking down onto the Kikuchi River that flows majestically through the urban areas of Tamana City, and in the distance you can see as far as the Ariake Sea. On the third floor, the *hoshinoza* (star room) is a space for experiencing the portents of the future. Here a monument based on the motif of the lotus flower, the symbol of happiness, opens up toward the sky. The three arrows appearing to extend into space express the aspirations for the future development of Tamana City.

Night view from southwest

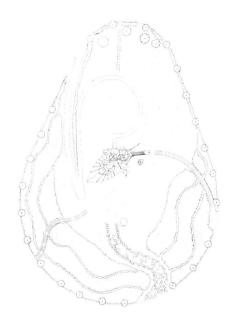

FACING PAGE *View from northeast*
ABOVE *Site plan*
LEFT *Overall view from west*

FACING PAGE *Detail of southwest facade*
RIGHT *View of south entry stair*
FAR RIGHT *View of south facade*
BELOW *Worm's-eye view of southwest facade*

FACING PAGE *View of north facade*
BELOW LEFT *View of boat-shaped plaza and space of zero*
BELOW CENTER *Exterior of space of zero*
BELOW RIGHT *Entrance to space of zero*

FACING PAGE BELOW *Top of space of zero*
LEFT *Detail of northeast facade*
BELOW *Structure based on lotus flowers*

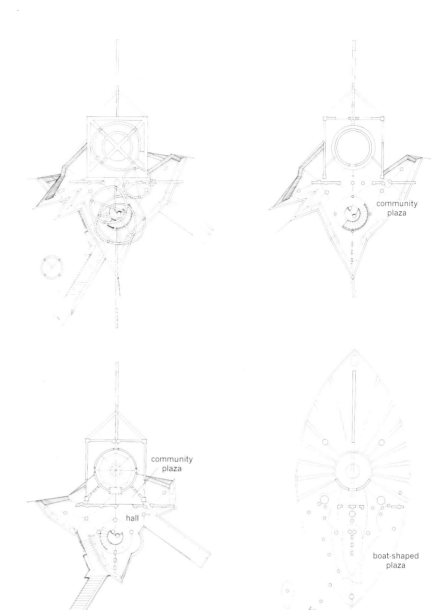

THIS PAGE
TOP LEFT *Roof plan*
TOP RIGHT *Third floor plan*
BOTTOM LEFT *Second floor plan*
BOTTOM RIGHT *First floor plan*

FACING PAGE
ABOVE LEFT *West elevation*
ABOVE RIGHT *South elevation*
LEFT *West section*

FOLLOWING PAGES
Interiors of space of zero

community
plaza

community
plaza

hall

boat-shaped
plaza

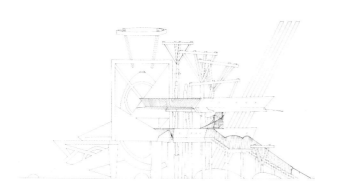

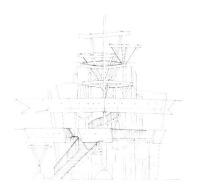

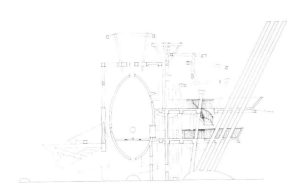

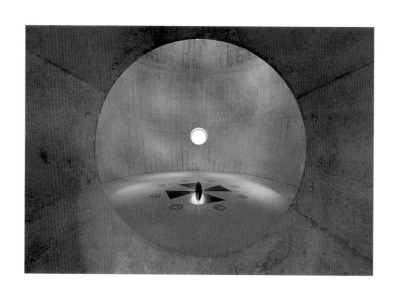

EARTH ARCHITECTURE

Hoya-shi
Tokyo-to
1994

The Earth Architecture housing complex was built ten years after its basic idea had been proposed. In many of my works, I conceive my ideas before I am commissioned for a particular site and type of building. The foundation of my style is to express my expectations for the development of society and the passage of time with architecture.

I am perplexed that Earth Architecture, which is based on a ten-year-old idea, is even now described as "futuristic" or "curious." The form of Earth Architecture is a crystallization of shapes of thought, which have to be included in architecture. An architectural concept can be made highly conscious of beauty by thinking and considering why a building has to be built at a given site. Architecture that is not as worthy as art cannot influence society, and architecture that is void of influential energy cannot be presented as art. I am engaged in bringing both artistry and socialization to architecture.

In the case of Earth Architecture, I tried to make a housing complex open to the public so as to lead communications and relationships within the community. Because of the appearance of public houses, several problems have occurred in many Japanese neighborhoods, symbolized by the breakdown of the community in overpopulated cities. Typical planning such as a "2DK" (two bedrooms, dining room, and kitchen) or "3LDK" (three bedrooms, living room, dining room, and kitchen) limits the lifestyle of its inhabitants. People believe that the arrangement of private rooms will allow them to increase their individuality, but it has done so to the point of isolating or estranging the individual from their neighbors or family. In designing Earth Architecture, I tried to promote a familiar human community within each family's separate apartment, among the fifteen families of the complex, and (by sharing the public space) within the neighborhood.

From Earth Architecture Mount Fuji can be seen in the west. The eternal view of Mount Fuji does not change over time. Instead it is a symbol of the

Night view of public steps

area, a symbol that produces solidarity among its inhabitants. I thought of Earth Architecture as a mountain; in the future, this architecture could be covered with plant life so that people would be able to participate in the change in nature and the change of seasons. I designed the building to show the passage of time.

The public space is large compared to that of a typical ready-made housing complex. Much of it, such as the community room (house of zero cosmology) at the top, is open to the neighborhood. In a typical complex, the main passage would exist only for residents. However, in this case, the path/plaza is not only for the inhabitants but for their neighbors. Similarly, the stairs that go to the roof garden could be used as seats during local festivals or as play structures for children. The roof garden, an "opened" area for a "closed" part of the building, helps people grow independent in an unrestricted place.

In Earth Architecture, the private spaces for fifteen families allow varying lifestyles and balance individuality with relationships with others. I created spaces like "cosmology of fire," "cosmology of water," and a bowed wall to give motion to the space of daily life. I arranged movable partition doors to allow adaptability for inhabitants' changing lifestyles.

I believe that Earth Architecture, together with its natural surroundings and the human community of the area, will give birth to a new conception of "hometown" and will show that housing complexes can be places in which to live a holistic life.

LEFT *Aerial view*
BELOW *View from north*

BELOW *View of south facade; the third floor terrace can be used as a stage set*

FOLLOWING PAGES
LEFT *Sunset view of sky plaza*
RIGHT *Night view of south facade*

RIGHT *View up from ground plaza*
FAR RIGHT *View from third floor to ground plaza*
BELOW *Detail of northwest corner*

LEFT *View down from sky plaza*
BELOW *Letter of Man on ground plaza*

FACING PAGE *Pole penetrating through the west vegetable garden*
LEFT *View from private community plaza*
BELOW *View up public steps from north*

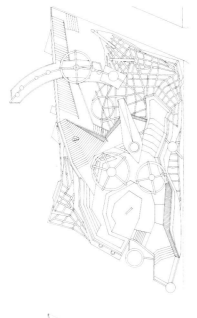
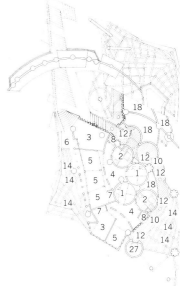

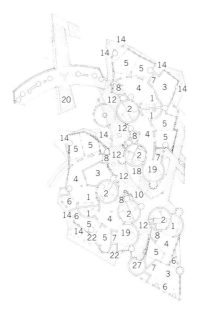

TOP *Site, attic, and fourth floor plans*
BOTTOM *Third floor, second floor, and first floor plans*

KEY
1 *Cosmology of fire* (kitchen)
2 *Cosmology of water* (bathroom)
3 *Parents' room*
4 *Family room*
5 *Private room*
6 *Terrace*
7 *Closet*
8 *Entrance*
9 *Ground plaza*
10 *Private community plaza*
11 *Cosmology of gate*
12 *Stepping stone*
13 *Rabbit wall*

14 *Garden*
15 *Mechanical room*
16 *Bicycle parking*
17 *Utility room*
18 *Void*
19 *Cosmology of man* (tatami *room*)
20 *Public steps*
21 *Floating bridge*
22 *Skylight*
23 *Sky plaza*
24 *House of zero cosmology* (community room)
25 *Bench*
26 *Earthman*
27 *Elevator*

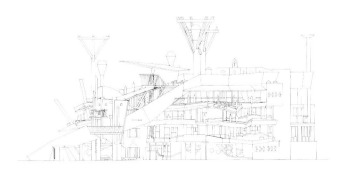

ABOVE LEFT *South elevation*
ABOVE RIGHT *West elevation*
LEFT *Section*

FOLLOWING PAGES
LEFT *Public steps to sky plaza*
RIGHT *Exterior wall of first floor private
community plaza and rabbit wall*

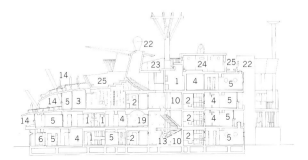

LEFT *View of second floor private community plaza*
BELOW *Entrance of apartment 101*

Interiors of apartment 301

FACING PAGE *Cosmology of man (tatami room) in apartment 204*
LEFT *Interior of community room on sky plaza*
BELOW *Cosmology of fire (kitchen) and cosmology of water (bathroom) in apartment 304*

ASO·KUJU NATIONAL
PARK RESTAURANT

Kuju·cho, Naoiri·gun
Oita·ken
1994

The Aso-Kuju National Park Restaurant stands in a beautiful natural site at 1100 meters above sea level, in front of the Kuju Mountains, looking at the Aso Mountains ahead. The theme of this design is how to exist as a landmark in a natural environment. I tried to cooperate with the ecology of the site while creating a strong impression within it. My planning concept was to bring people together with nature and to express nature by mixing exterior and interior spaces. The energy of each shape of the building, flowing from exterior to interior or from interior to exterior, connects this architecture with the mountains and contributes to a good mutual stimulation between architecture and nature.

The client wanted to create a high-quality "amusement cosmology" at the site. The restaurant was to express an elegant urbanity, which guests can experience by walking around, as if in a theater, taking in views of the mountains. Architecture in national parks, even such details as form, material, and color, is designed under the strict regulations of Japan's Environmental Agency.

I attempted to draw people to the highland restaurant with careful consideration and sensitive feelings. My creative efforts focused on planning the flow of the exterior and the color scheme of the interior. I cannot describe the beauty of the sunset that changes the Kuju highlands into a blue-purple. More or less because I felt the beauty of the color, I chose a blue-purple color scheme for the interior. The colors of the interior flow with those of the exterior, as if in a rhythm.

An "amusement cosmology" suitable for the environment of the site would not be created if it did not retain the nature of the Kuju highlands and reflect the beauty of the scenery as it changes with time.

The experience of nature is not realizable by solely viewing scenery from big windows.

View up into void

BELOW *View from south*
FACING PAGE *View of southwest facade with*
Kuju Mountain in the background

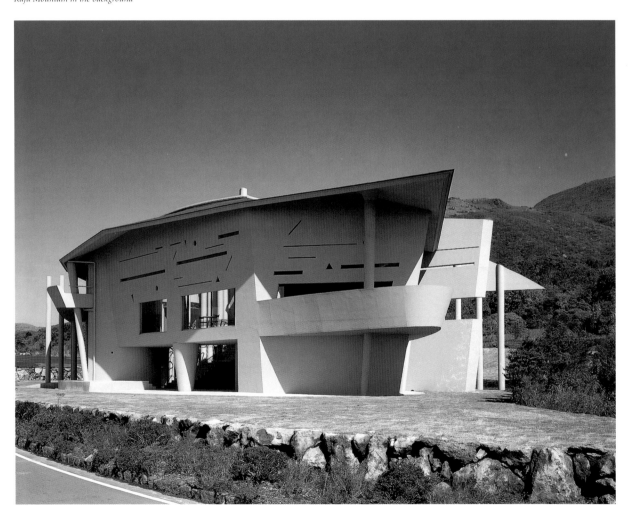

FACING PAGE *Entrance*
FAR LEFT *Detail of southwest facade*
LEFT *View from southeast approach*
BELOW *East facade*

FOLLOWING PAGES
LEFT *Night view from northwest*
RIGHT *Night view from north*

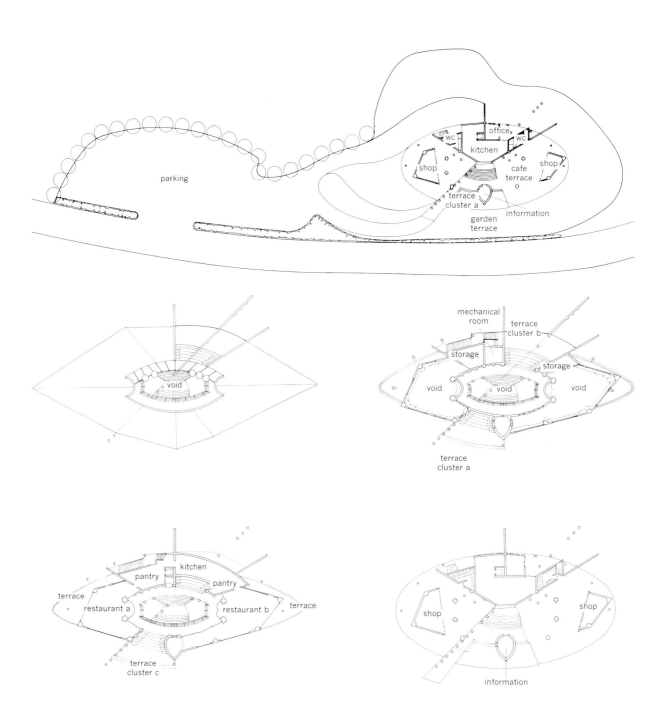

FACING PAGE
TOP *Site plan*
CENTER LEFT *Roof plan*
CENTER RIGHT *Third floor plan*
BOTTOM LEFT *Second floor plan*
BOTTOM RIGHT *First floor plan*

THIS PAGE
TOP LEFT *Southeast elevation*
TOP RIGHT *Southwest elevation*
BOTTOM *Southeast section*

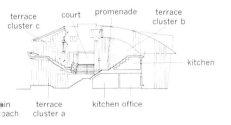

terrace cluster c   court   promenade   terrace cluster b

kitchen

main beach   terrace cluster a   kitchen office

FACING PAGE *View of void from restaurant b*
RIGHT *View into void*
BELOW *View of terrace cluster b from terrace cluster c*

FACING PAGE *Interior of restaurant a*
LEFT *View of restaurant b from central steps*
BELOW *View of Aso Mountains from restaurant b*

RIGHT *View of restaurant a at sunset*
BELOW *Interior of restaurant a*
FACING PAGE *Interior of restaurant b*

KIHOKU
ASTRONOMICAL MUSEUM

Ichinari, Kihoku-cho
Kagoshima-ken
1995

The Kihoku Astronomical Museum stands at Kihoku-cho, a town of approximately 4800 inhabitants. Kihoku-cho has experienced problems because of a large emigration of people; a great proportion of its residences are seniors. But the natural environment of this town is very beautiful. It lies in the mountains, and has received an award for "the most beautiful night skies of Japan in summer and winter" in the Nationwide Continuous Observatory Contest organized by Japan's Environmental Agency. The essential theme of this project is to give new life to the town by addressing the beautiful night skies.

The site of the Kihoku Astronomical Museum is in the Kihoku Uwaba Park. At 550 meters above sea level, the place offers views of Sakurajima Island, a living volcano, and Kinko Bay to the west, Miyakonojo Basin to the east, Kirishima Mountains to the north, and Shibushi Bay to the south. Such beautiful scenes fascinated me, and I strongly felt that this site was the most suitable place to communicate with the museum. Architecture lives together with its site—here both that of the land and that of space. The crystallized geometry of the area is reflected in the museum.

The people of Kihoku-cho enjoy communicating with the architecture and with the cosmos as framed by the architecture. Because the museum has received media coverage and a large number of visitors, the people of Kihoku-cho are experiencing sensations that they have not felt before. It is a great pleasure, as an architect, to be able to contribute to the life of the local society of this town.

It is a pleasure to create architecture that will be at the center of a local society. I felt the social role of architecture much deeper when I met the exciting situation of Kihoku-cho through the Kihoku Astronomical Museum. At its place of construction, architecture can be a living body that shows the power of its presence when it has been created with joy.

View of the observation plaza from the southeast

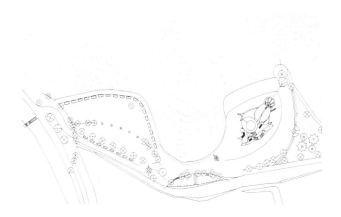

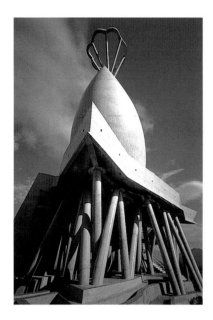

FAR LEFT *View from northwest*
LEFT *View of gate*
BELOW *View from southeast; the observatory room and the exhibition room are supported by independent columns*

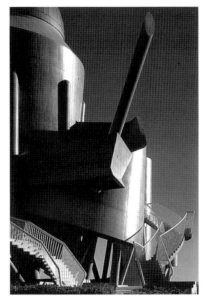

FACING PAGE
Detail of stairs

THIS PAGE
LEFT *Detail view of east facade*
CENTER *Detail view of south facade*
RIGHT *Detail of stairs*

FOLLOWING PAGES
LEFT *Star theater on the second floor*
RIGHT *View of auditorium and observation
plaza from east*

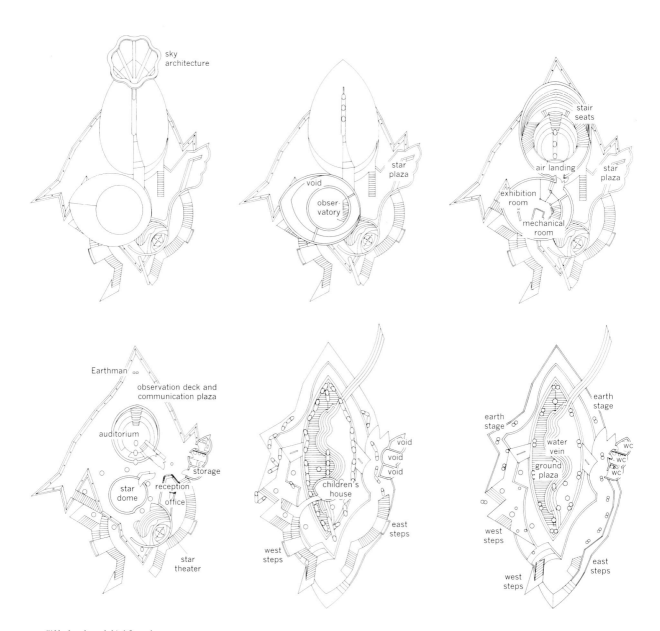

sky
architecture

void

obser-
vatory

star
plaza

stair
seats

air landing

exhibition
room

mechanical
room

star
plaza

Earthman

observation deck and
communication plaza

auditorium

storage

star
dome

reception

office

star
theater

void
void
void

children's
house

east
steps

west
steps

earth
stage

earth
stage

water
vein

ground
plaza

wc
wc
wc

west
steps

west
steps

east
steps

TOP *Fifth, fourth, and third floor plans*
BOTTOM *Second, mezzanine, and first*
floor plans

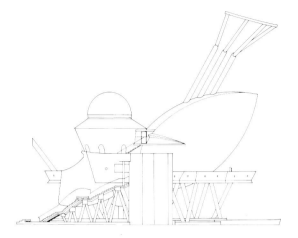

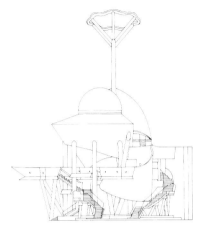

ABOVE LEFT *Northeast elevation*
ABOVE RIGHT *Southeast elevation*
LEFT *Northeast section*

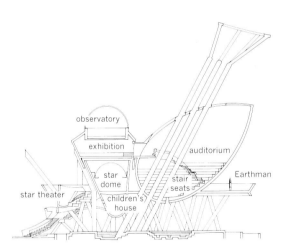

observatory

exhibition

auditorium

star dome

star seats

Earthman

star theater

children's house

FACING PAGE *Ground plaza*
LEFT *View down toward ground plaza*
BELOW *View of Sakurajima Island from ground plaza*

LEFT *Earthman and auditorium stand on observation plaza*
BELOW *View from observation plaza toward auditorium*
FACING PAGE *View up into auditorium; the pillars pierce through the ceiling into the sky*

RIGHT *Axonometric of auditorium*
FAR RIGHT *Entrance to auditorium*
BELOW *Interior of auditorium*

LEFT *Detail of stair seats in auditorium*
BELOW *View down into auditorium*

SHOMYO KINDERGARTEN

Mizobe-cho
Kagoshima-ken
1995

With the changes to contemporary society, the presence of kindergartens is needed as a regional social institution to help children grow and to reconstruct a sense of community. This project attempts to address how a piece of architecture can affect quality of life.

Shomyo Kindergarten plays the dual role of an information center for regional culture (specifically its neighbor, the Shomyo Temple) and a kindergarten. The location of this project, Mizobe-cho in Kagoshima-ken, has both modern aspects, like an airport that acts as an entrance to southern Japan, and historical aspects, because Amatsuhidakahikohohodeminomikoto (Yamasachihiko), an ancestor of Emperor Shinmu, is deified and buried here at Kouokusanjouryou (a big tomb akin to a hill).

There are a tea garden and various trees around the site. The nature of the place is unique, and I thought that I had to build an original architecture for such a site. I designed this kindergarten to encourage the children in activities like finding native forms, feeling color, and forming their inherent natures.

In addition I designed this architecture to make children's inborn independence grow by promoting adventure in the site and the space plan. The culture and life of children is playing. The space receives children's impulsive energy, so I used circles, triangles, squares, and spirals as the basis of the design because they can stimulate children's creative impulses or instill calm. These forms are found in the natural environment. I adopted an elevated-floor style, an architectural form found in Kagoshima, and used it in the Japanese Samgharama style like that used in the Shomyo Temple. The central dome is an egg shape from Kouokusanjouryou; with its office and kitchen wings, it forms the image of an airplane. The whole shape of the building is a child lying and stretching his arms and feet. This figure is a cosmogram that signifies a child calling the sky.

View of domed hall built on elevated floor

RIGHT *View of south facade from tea garden*
BELOW *View from west*
FACING PAGE *Detail of south facade and domed hall*

ABOVE RIGHT *Night view from north; the building serves as a community center at night and for holidays*
RIGHT *View of entrance; a room for two year olds is on the left of the square plaza, while a room for children one year old and younger is on the right*
FACING PAGE *Exterior of a room for children one year old and younger*

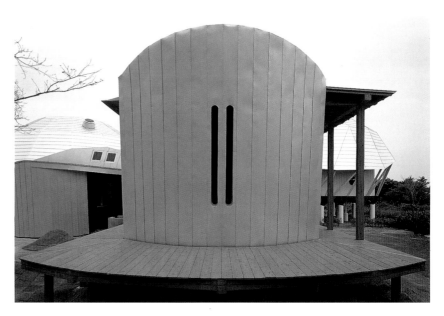

RIGHT *View from west*
BELOW *View from east*

LEFT *View from south; the roof and light structures are landmarks in the town (Shomyo Temple is to the left)*
BELOW *Detail of various roof shapes*

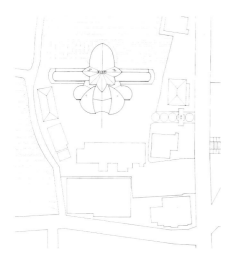

ABOVE *Site plan*
RIGHT *Roof, gallery, and first floor plans*

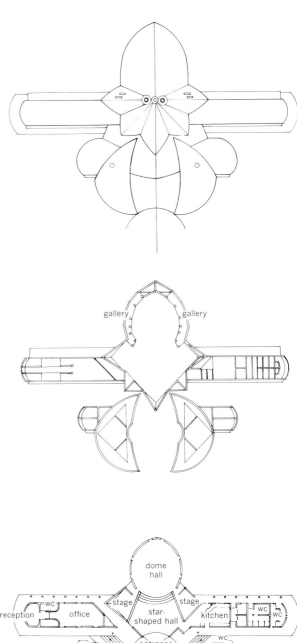

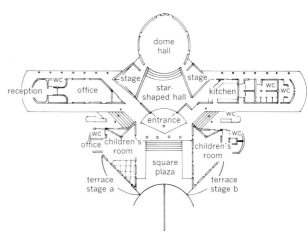

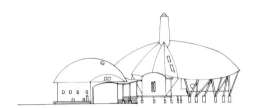

TOP *North elevation*
CENTER *West elevation*
BOTTOM *West section*

FOLLOWING PAGES
LEFT *View of entrance hall from room for children one year old and younger*
RIGHT *Entrance hall; interior joints meet exterior joints*

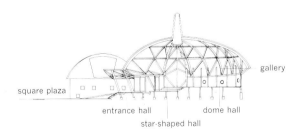

square plaza

entrance hall

star-shaped hall

dome hall

gallery

RIGHT *Interior of room for two year olds*
BELOW *View of rest room from children's room*

RIGHT *View of teacher's room from entrance hall*
BELOW *Interior of teacher's room*

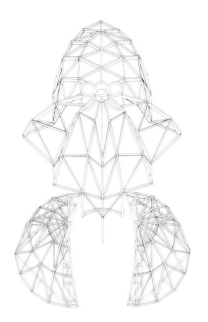

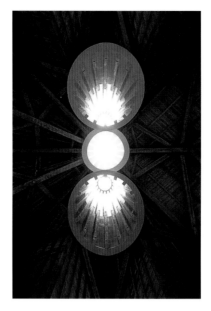

ABOVE LEFT *Axonometric of wooden roof structure*
ABOVE CENTER *Detail of lights above dome hall*
ABOVE RIGHT *Interior of dome hall*
RIGHT *Ceremony in dome hall*
FACING PAGE *View of dome hall from star-shaped hall*

TAKASAKI MASAHARU
MUSEUM OF ARCHITECTURE

Ibusuki-shi
Kagoshima-ken
1996

The southern section of Kyushu Island, which is one of my working places, faces several bodies of water. The East China Sea, the South China Sea, the Indian Ocean, the Arabian Sea, and the Mediterranean Sea link up in the interchanging area of marine culture that I have called "The Ocean Silk Road." From Ibusuki-shi one can see the active volcano of Sakurajima Island far away and the dormant volcano of Mount Kaimondake close by at the tip of Satsuma Peninsula. Ibusuki-shi is symbolic of southern Kagoshima; the city has the rich and peculiar character of the south.

The Takasaki Masaharu Museum of Architecture is the third project in the series Kagoshima Cosmology of Architecture, architectural projects for the Ocean Silk Road. (The Kihoku Astronomical Museum and the Shomyo Kindergarten are the first two projects in the series.) The series promotes a network of architectural culture in southern Kyushu. The architectural forms of these projects symbolically express the regional identity that derives from the history, nature, and culture formed by dialogues among the many civilizations on the Ocean Silk Road. By planning an area to connect individual architecture, a broad lively space would be formed. It would lead visitors to the network of Kagoshima and its memorable scenery. I hope that focusing on the scenery in a local community leads to a change or reconstruction of the community's sense of values.

The museum explores the color of the deep ocean. It also explores the relationships between society and architecture from the point of view of a culture residing with its public character. Here complete architectures and new projects can be presented. The museum is also a place for studying city planning and the education of people for the animation of local societies.

In future projects of the Kagoshima Cosmology of Architecture, I will search for an opportunity to meet the idea of each native climate or civilization on the Ocean Silk Road.

East facade showing the wall as an abstract picture

RIGHT *View from north*
BELOW *View from northeast*
FACING PAGE *Detail of north facade*

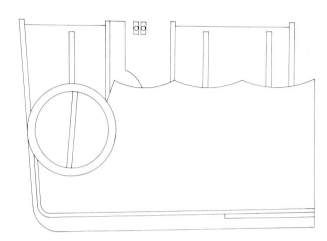

Uomidake

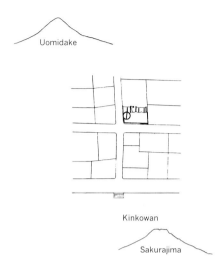

Kinkowan

Sakurajima

LEFT *Site plan*
RIGHT *Roof, second, and first floor plans*

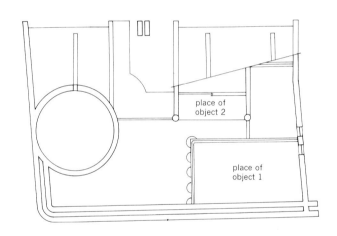

place of object 2

place of object 1

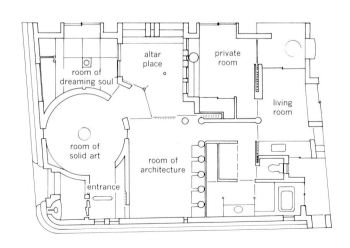

room of dreaming soul

altar place

private room

living room

room of solid art

room of architecture

entrance

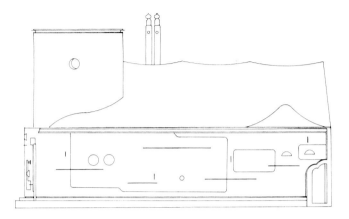

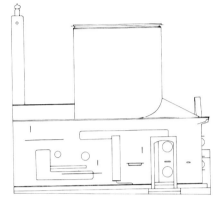

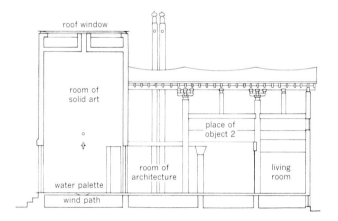

roof window

room of
solid art

place of
object 2

room of
architecture

living
room

water palette

wind path

ABOVE LEFT *North elevation*
ABOVE RIGHT *East elevation*
LEFT *North section*

ABOVE LEFT *Stone for taking off one's shoes;*
figures on the stone symbolically express the
concept of the museum
ABOVE RIGHT *Wash bowl at entrance;*
sunlight reflects from the bowl and spreads
over the glass ceiling
RIGHT *View through entry door, based on*
the motif of a human body, to entrance hall
FACING PAGE *View of entrance hall, which is*
a prologue to the room of solid art

Room of solid art; the room is shaped like a pot, which means blessings from nature and communication with heaven

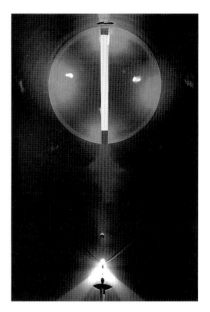

ABOVE LEFT *Water palette made of emerald pearl; it expresses a blessed life and rebirth*
ABOVE CENTER *Detail of a wall in room of dreaming soul*
ABOVE RIGHT *View to ceiling of room of solid art*
LEFT *Interior of room of solid art*

FOLLOWING PAGES
LEFT *Figure based on the shape of a finger; it expresses a spiritual, philosophical essence*
RIGHT *The room of the dreaming soul expresses the deep spirit in architecture*

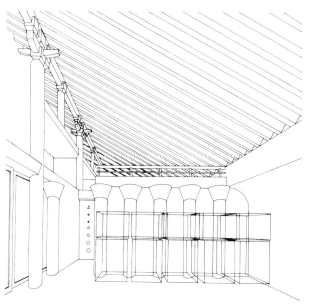

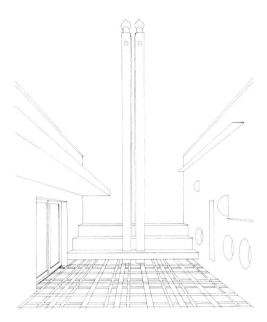

FACING PAGE
TOP LEFT *View of room of architecture,
which contains symbolic forms of the coun-
tries of the Ocean Silk Road*
TOP RIGHT *Drawing of room of architecture*
BOTTOM *Room of architecture*

THIS PAGE
TOP *Drawing of altar place*
BOTTOM *View of altar place from room of
architecture*

LEFT *View of well from private room*
BELOW *View of private room*
FACING PAGE *View of wall and fountain on terrace*

PROJECTS

ENERGY EARTH
Nagoya-shi, Aichi-ken, 1988

ABOVE *View of entrance from south*
RIGHT *View up from entry corridor*

FAR LEFT *View from staircase to inner plaza*
LEFT *The fabric of the inner plaza, which is the place for communication with the neighborhood*
BELOW *Composition of inner plaza*

COSMOS OF CHIZU
Tottori-shi, Tottori-ken, 1991

ABOVE *View of southeast facade*
RIGHT *Entrance*

FAR LEFT *Corridor*
LEFT *Arch above corridor*
BELOW *View of terrace from living room*

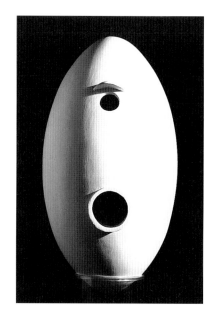
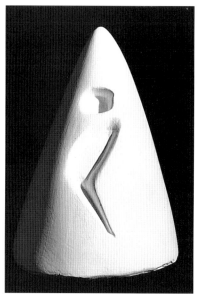
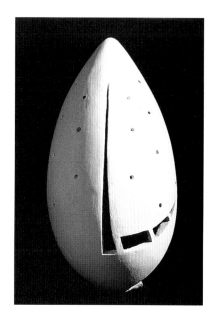
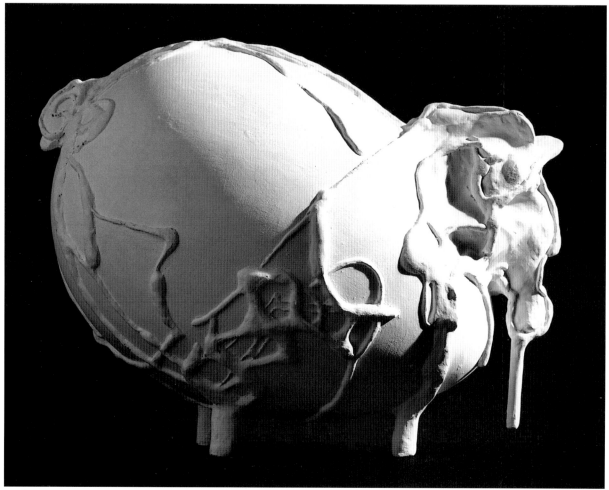

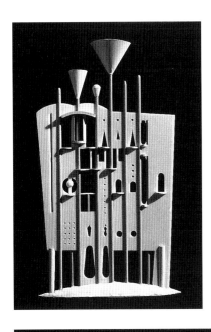

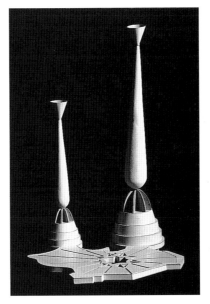

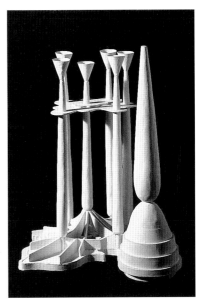

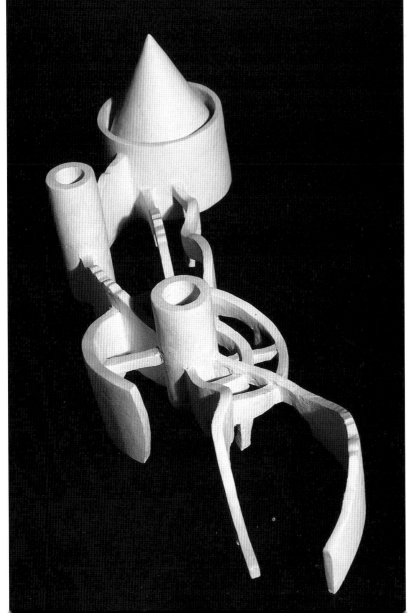

FACING PAGE
TOP LEFT *Zero Form—The Moon*
(auditorium), 1985
TOP CENTER *Urform—Fire*
(auditorium), 1985
TOP RIGHT *Zero Form—Lightening*
(auditorium), 1986
BOTTOM *Earthian*
(residence and office), 1972

THIS PAGE
TOP LEFT *Cosmogram*
(high-rise building), 1985
TOP CENTER *Twins in Utopia*
(high-rise building), 1990
TOP RIGHT *Crowd in Utopia*
(high-rise building), 1990
BOTTOM *Flow Form*
(building complex), 1985

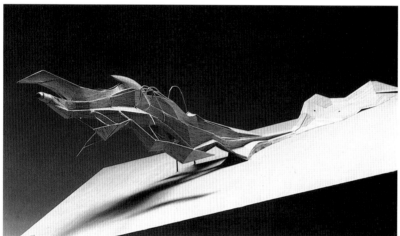

TOP *Earthian Heart*
(cultural and commercial complex), 1987
CENTER *Flight of Power*
(residence and office), 1980
BOTTOM *Layer of Echo*
(cultural and commercial complex), 1983

TOP *Sunbathing*
(residence and kindergarten), 1987
CENTER *The Moon*
(residence, atelier, and theater), 1978
BOTTOM *The Sun*
(residence, atelier, and theater), 1982

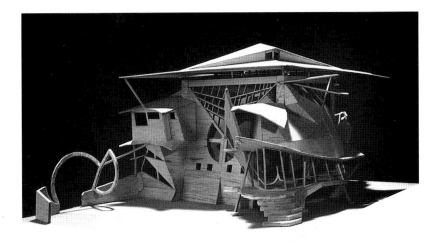

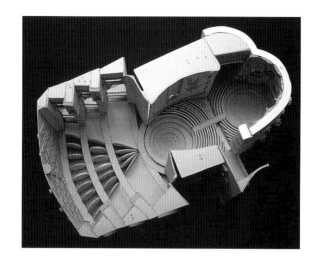

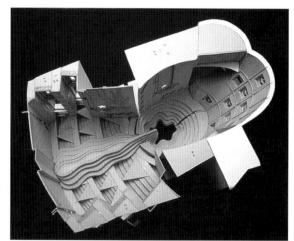

THIS PAGE *Studies of private room, 1987*
FACING PAGE *The Human*
(building complex), 1984

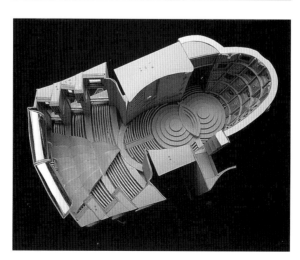

FACING PAGE
Earth, Water, Fire, and Wind exhibition (installation), 1990

THIS PAGE
ABOVE LEFT *Casper Experimental Theater, 1984*
ABOVE *Probability (installation)*, 1990
LEFT *Inviting Door*, 1984

LIST OF WORKS

The Social Formative Arts—architecture as a place where people encounter and communicate with one another; architecture that positively makes environmental spaces

1982 The Sun (residence, atelier, and theater)—a polyhedral structure for the rest and refreshment of the soul

1983 The Earth (lodging)—an attempt to make an architectural structure in the shape of the Earth so as to be a part of nature

1983 Bundle of Light (condominium)

1983 Layer of Echo (cultural and commercial complex)—a symphony of forms exploring various types of places and spaces

1984 The Air Package (restaurant)

1984 The Layer of Air Flow (museum)

1984 The Human (building complex)

1984 The Earth '84 (museum)

1986 The Earth '86 (department store)—a structure that envelops the breadth and height of the Earth, the liveliness of light, the warmth of a palm, and mounting excitement

1987 Crystal Light, Shibuya-ku, Tokyo-to (residence and office)

1987 Sunbathing (residence and kindergarten)—a familiar form made in emotional colors that inspire children's senses ; a smiling architecture

1987 The Earth '87 (commercial establishment)—a dynamic form of an exploding Earth

1987 The Globe (office)

1988 Layer of Echo, Kagoshima (cultural complex)

1989 Phases of Echo, Nagoya (residence)

1989 Okasan Securities Makuhari Branch, Makuhari, Chiba-shi, Chiba-ken (office)

1991 Cosmos of Chizu, Tottori-shi, Tottori-ken (residence)

1994 Earth Architecture, Hoya-shi, Tokyo-to (condominium)—a house as a magnetic field for various social functions; the design takes into account the natural and peculiar history and customs of native residents

1994 Kihokucho Mother of Star (exhibition area and study room)

1994 Kihokucho Star House (lodging)

1994 Aso-Kuju National Park Restaurant, Kuju-cho, Naoiri-gun, Oita-ken (restaurant)

1995 Roadside Station in the Town of Aga, Rakui-chi-Jipangu, Mikawa-mura, Niigata-ken (shopping complex, fish market)

1995 Osumi Police Box, Kihoku-cho, Kagoshima-ken

1996 Town of Flowers, Hot Springs, and Communication, Kinpo-cho, Kagoshima-ken

1996 Sapporo Kindergarten, Sapporo-shi

1996 Natural Park Sakamoto, Sakamoto-mura, Kumamoto-ken

The Individual in Space—the space to communicate with oneself or to meditate; the architecture inspires individual spirits and senses through progressive communication between things and humans

1991 Zero Cosmology, Kagoshima-shi, Kagoshima-ken (residence)

1994 Japanese Tea Ceremony Room of Steal, Kitakyushi-shi, Fukuoka-ken

1994 Japanese Tea Ceremony Room of Aluminum, Toyama, Toyama-ken

1994 U-Hospital, Koyama-cho, Kagoshima-ken

1996 Takasaki Masaharu Museum of Architecture, Ibusuki-shi, Kagoshima-ken (museum and residence)

The Universal Formative Art—architecture that helps discover the essence of relationships between the cosmos and people

1991 Uchinoura Town Hall, Uchinoura-cho, Kagoshima-ken

1992 Tamana City Observatory Museum, Tamana, Kumamoto-ken (observatory and hall)

1995 Kihoku Astronomical Museum, Kihoku-cho, Kagoshima-ken (astronomical observatory and hall)

1995 Shomyo Kindergarten, Mizobe-cho, Kagoshima-ken